An Introduction to
MOUNTAIN BIKING

An Introduction to
MOUNTAIN BIKING

Brant Richards

This 2000 edition is published by
Gramercy Books™, an imprint of
Random House Value Publishing, Inc.,
280 Park Avenue, New York,
NY 10017

Gramercy Books™ and design are
trademarks of Random House Value
Publishing, Inc.

Random House
New York • Toronto • London •
Sydney • Auckland

http://www.randomhouse.com/

Printed in Italy

ISBN 0-517-16165-6

10 9 8 7 6 5 4 3 2 1

Contents

Chapter One
What to Ride?

Although bicycles all share basically the same characteristics – a wheel at each end, handlebars, a saddle, pedals and the means for making the bike go forward – how these components are arranged, what they look like, and how they all fit together can differ a great deal depending on the purpose for which the bike will be used.

Nowadays, the mountain bike is the most common type sold. The average cyclist has largely abandoned 'racing look-alike' machines, swapping their cramped riding position and low-slung dropped handlebars for the straight-barred 'see where you're going' position of the mountain bike.

There are several features which distinguish the mountain bike from other types: a large substantial frame, chunkily treaded tyres, an upright riding position with a straight (not dropped) handlebar, powerful brakes – these are all typical features. But even within the whole gamut of mountain bikes, huge variations can still be found. Compare the almost motorbike

The mountain bike: with this, you can ride practically anywhere.

appearance of the modern downhill bike, with its long-travel suspension, high-speed gearing and disc brakes, with the light, almost flimsy construction of the cross-country racing bike. Enthusiasts of 'trail riding' bikes fall somewhere in between, borrowing components from each source and combining them into a bike that will provide the best of both worlds, but without having to compromise on efficiency. Let's start at the front and examine some of the bike's key parts.

Wheels

Every bike has wheels, though how they are constructed can vary from bike to bike; but the good old spoked wheel can still expect a long life, despite the advances of technology. Mountain-bike wheels have a 26-in (660-mm) outside diameter, with a tyre cross section of around 2in (51mm). Tyre size and tread pattern is dependent on how the bike will be used; usually, the harsher the terrain, the larger the tyre required.

The wheels usually consist of 32 or 36 spokes, laced to a hub and fixed to the front fork by means of a quick-release lever, which allows easy tool-free removal while out on the trail.

Forks

Suspension forks, or forks fitted with shock absorbers, like tiny motorbike forks, are rapidly becoming the norm on mountain bikes. They've been growing in popularity over the last ten years and with mass

manufacture and user acceptance now appear on almost all new bikes. The shock-absorbing action makes riding more comfortable, a benefit to both new and advanced riders alike. They fit into the frame via a headset, the steering bearings of which are fitted into the headtube of the bike. A stem clamps to the fork's steerer tube, running inside the bearings.

ABOVE: Rock Shox made the first suspension fork, and continue to dominate the market.

ABOVE LEFT: Mountain bikes have knobbly tyres to provide efficient traction in all conditions.

LEFT: Wheels are lightweight, despite their strength and chunky appearance.

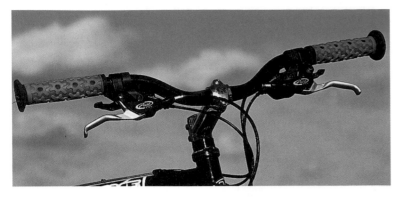

Handlebars

Although traditional straight bars are fitted to most mountain bikes, more and more are now being sold with 'riser' bars, handlebars with a small S-bend at each side, lifting the bar above the stem to give a more comfortable riding position. Neither has any huge advantage over the other, it is a question of the rider being at ease on the bike. Riser bars can be fitted instead of straight bars to give extra rise and a more comfortable upright riding position. Some riders prefer to use a high-rise stem to give the extra height,

but it really makes little difference. Riser bars are usually available in a wider size, which gives a more comfortable position: but you must try to keep a sense of proportion.

Frames

Because there are so many different manufacturers, frame materials, construction techniques and designs, hardly any two mountain bikes manage to look the same, though all do the same basic job, providing a mounting point for the handlebars, pedals, saddle, forks and rear wheel. Traditional frames are made from tubular aluminium

TOP FAR LEFT: Riser bars have a gentle bend to give a comfortable riding position.

TOP LEFT: Straight bars are still popular, especially for faster riding.

CENTRE LEFT: A traditional frameset, built in modern materials.

BELOW LEFT: Full suspension framesets give a superior ride on uneven surfaces, but are not strictly necessary.

TOP RIGHT: Disc brakes efficiently slow you down in all conditions.

TOP FAR RIGHT: Detail of brake action.

RIGHT: A hydraulic disc brake.

FAR RIGHT: Flat pedals that grip well help keep your feet in place.

BELOW: With three chainrings to choose from, gearing looks complex but in fact is not.

BELOW CENTRE: The Shimano XTR rear mech.

BELOW RIGHT: Toe clips have given way to clipless pedals.

or steel, welded into a 'double-diamond' configuration; but as techniques alter and rear suspension becomes more common, traditional designs are becoming rarer.

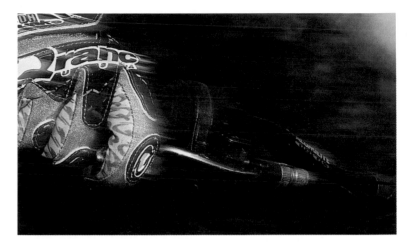

The Chainset and Front Mech

This is where your leg power gets transferred to the bike. The chainset has three chainrings which give different gear ratios, the ratios being selected by the front mech, which moves the chain from ring to ring.

The Rear Mech and Cassette

The gears at the back of the bike are controlled by the rear mech. Seven, eight or nine sprockets mounted on a freewheeling cassette at the rear wheel give the corresponding number of gear ratios. Altogether, a mountain bike can have up to 27 different gears.

Brakes

Actuated by cables, pulled by levers on the bars, most mountain bikes use rim-acting brakes. More expensive machines may use disc brakes to slow the bike down more efficiently, which can either be cable or more usually hydraulically controlled.

Pedals

Two types are in common use which include a standard flat pedal with an aggressive pattern, usually referred to as a 'flat' pedal, and a pedal with a mechanical 'ski-binding' system, which clips to a compatible shoe via a metal cleat bolted into the shoe's sole. These are called 'clipless' pedals by virtue of the fact

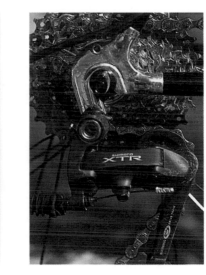

that they replace flat pedals with toe clips. The irony is that clipless pedals have made toe clips largely obsolete, so that the flat pedals they were mounted on are now 'clipless', a fact which confuses most mountain bikers.

Most beginners' bikes come with a flat pedal, some occasionally with toe clips. More advanced bikes will come with a more aggressive flat pedal, or clipless pedal. Some expensive bikes come without pedals at all, not to cut back on price, but because riders at the top end of the market tend to become quite obsessive about them and like to make their own selection.

Saddles and Seat Posts

The saddle is fixed to the frame by a seat post, also known as a seat pin, which fits into the seat tube of the bike. Don't confuse these terms, otherwise you will be an innocent source of amusement at the bike shop.

Cross-Country Racing

A bike selected for this purpose must be light and strong – light so the rider has no excess weight to cope with while he's trying to keep up with the field, and strong so that the bike finishes in one piece. A saying among racers is that to finish first, first you've got to finish.

Race courses for mountain bikes largely dictate the type of bike used. Over the years, however, the severity of these courses has been somewhat modified, and as a result bikes have become lighter and more like their road-bike cousins.

The frame, the heart of the

bike, is designed to be stiff and strong, yet as light as possible. Obviously, money is no object at the higher levels of

professional racing and dream materials such as carbon fibre, titanium and aerospace aluminium can be used, along

LEFT: Set your seat height so that you are going to feel comfortable for as long as possible.

OPPOSITE: Cross-country racers don't mind putting their bodies through hell to get a good result. However, you don't need to take matters to such extremes.

BELOW: Lightly treaded 'semi-slick' tyres were developed for the racers, but work well on all terrains with all riders.

BOTTOM: Biking pioneer Gary Fisher's superlight 'Sugar' suspension bike costs a fortune but goes like a dream.

cross-country events is the semi-slick tyre which, at first glance, appears to be worn out, but has a very smooth tread and barely noticeable knobbles on their sides to aid cornering in loose conditions.

While suspension bikes (those with a rear shock absorber) have made inroads into cross-country racing, the majority of riders still use traditional rigid bikes which can weigh 2lb (1kg) less. Suspension forks are common, though these will usually be lightweight air-sprung models with small amounts (1–2in/2.5–5cm) of travel.

Handlebars and stems on cross-country race bikes are usually similar to those on road bikes in a position that many casual riders might find uncomfortable. Stems are long and low and handlebars narrow to force the rider into an aerodynamic position so that he can slice cleanly through the air. Technical handling on rough surfaces is usually compromised, but with many cross-country races taking place on rolling terrain, rather than rocky, twisty, technical tracks, it's a fact of life that riders live with. Even though race courses are usually all riding, sections may include stream crossings and some dismounting over obstacles.

Tyres are minimally treaded, narrow in section and pumped up hard: these riders can manage to live without the comfort factor of fatter, heavier-treaded tyres even though they've been racing for a couple of hours.

with highly refined steel alloys and other wonder metals. Bikes will often be truly custom-built to fit the rider, rather like a well tailored bespoke suit, when

their personal measurements and preferences will be taken into account, and a frame built specifically to their requirements. In fact, in the quest for excellence, there is

almost no end to the amount of money that is spent.

Racing provides the impetus for new products to be developed, and one notable innovation from fast

During the course of a race, be prepared to encounter many and varied obstacles, including running water!

Trail Bikes

For purely recreational riding, it is clearly obvious that budgets won't stretch as far as they do for the pro race circuit. However, even when it comes to riding around woods and trails, the trail bike should

still be expected to perform well in every situation. Depending on the terrain, different adjustments will need to be made: indeed, in select pockets around the world there are riders whose bikes are set up quite uniquely because of the terrain they habitually encounter, with short, steep stems to kick back the riding position for steep downhills, large-diameter knobbly tyres to soak up rocky terrain, or with padding on the bike to allow it to be carried. Whatever the local terrain dictates, the rider will usually find the bike that suits him best. As a result, there is no definitive trail bike, only a few criteria to bear in mind.

Comfort is definitely an issue. Whereas a racer can and will put up with discomfort in pursuit of his goal, utilizing an uncomfortable but lightweight saddle and hard but fast-rolling tyres, the recreational rider is seeking pleasure, and consequently looks to a bike that's fun to ride, and comfortable into the bargain.

Fitting a saddle that doesn't feel like a razor blade is only the start. Suspension types are often chosen by recreational riders who are less likely to be obsessed by the extra pound or so that they weigh, and who will appreciate the added comfort after a long day in the saddle.

Tyres are chosen for grip, and also for the ease with which they handle the local terrain. Mud sticks, but the mud of different areas sticks in different ways. Trail riders seek tyres that work for their local terrain, gripping but not

OPPOSITE TOP: Gary Fisher practically invented the mountain bike and still has an active involvement in the sport.

OPPOSITE CENTRE: Don't put up with a saddle unless you're 100 per cent happy with it. WTB saddles are among the best around.

OPPOSITE BELOW: Riders out on the trail.

RIGHT: Trials riders call on their gymnastic skills to tackle tricky sections of the course.

BELOW: As a result, trials bikes are designed not for comfort, but for extreme manoeuvrability.

slipping, and certainly not changing into rolling doughnuts once the rain starts.

Gears are selected according to the terrain, and most of the time, except in exceptional circumstances, these will be left as supplied. If the locale has particularly steep climbs, then a more specialized form of equipment may be desirable.

Trials Bikes

Mountain-bike trials are all about riding over obstacles that would stop regular riders in their tracks. Trials bikes have small frames, powerful brakes and large tyres, all designed to help the rider achieve this object.

Trials mountain-bike riding developed from the sport of cyclo-trials, which itself was developed as a training aid for off-road motorcycle trials riders. Cyclo-trials bikes have 20-in (508-mm) wheels and BMX-sized frames, coupled with tall stems and wide handlebars. Mountain-bike trials machines have larger 26-in (660-mm) wheels, standard on all mountain bikes, but have the controls in a similar position.

Because of the nature of trialling, bikes have very low gears, usually provided by a small chainring at the front, and a compact cassette at the rear. The chainring is protected by the addition of a bash guard on the inside and outside of the chainring to protect the teeth from damage when the rider lands the bike on the chainrings, an approved technique, and inevitable when you're hopping over rocks and logs.

ABOVE: An expert rider clears a rocky track section with ease.

RIGHT: Magura hydraulic brakes are the trials rider's favourite.

Powerful brakes are needed to hold the bike on the front or back wheel. Most riders choose to use hydraulic rim brakes, such as those from Magura. A few riders use powerful disc brakes, but whatever the type, power is the main requisite. In order to hop and jump the bike over obstacles, the rider must be able to control the movement of the wheels, and lock them up instantly.

The saddle is set low in the frame to keep it out of the rider's way because they will usually be standing up, giving them a position powerful enough to move the bike from wheel to wheel over the obstacles.

The most important attribute needed by trials bikes is very strong wheels and tyres. These components take a real beating when the rider is jumping off rocks or negotiating large drops. Strong, wide rims and large knobbly trials-specific tyres are fitted to ensure cushioning, grip and strength.

Downhill Bikes

Mountain biking had its beginnings in downhilling: the origins of the sport and the industry that has developed from it can be traced to a group of riders who once met up to race down a mountain in Marin County, California, U.S.A.

Nowadays, downhill bikes bear so little resemblance to either the bikes that were ridden then, or the bikes that most recreational riders use now, that an almost different species has been created. Downhill bikes have developed purely for downhill use, and no compromises are made when it comes to riding back up the hill, unlike racing, where there's always a chairlift or truck to take you back to the top of the run for another go.

As a result, downhill bikes are heavy. They have to be in order to be strong. In fact, huge forks, powerful disc brakes, massive tyres and wide bars make the modern downhill bike look more like a motorbike than the mountain bikes that most riders use.

To emphasize the point, strength is what is most needed. With speeds reaching 50mph (80km) at times, over terrain that can be compared to a field strewn with boulders, downhill bikes must be designed so that both bike and rider survive. That strength has to come from somewhere, and is from the extra metal that's welded into the frame, and the braced frame designs that make the downhill bike what it is today.

Dual-crown suspension forks, which connect to the

top and bottom of the bike headtube, provide strength and stiffness, and the forks are designed to have up to 9in (229mm) of suspension compression. With rear swinging arms with coil-sprung oil-damped shock absorbers that reduce the punishment taken by the rear of the bike, these machines are like motorcycles without engines.

A single chainring is run, with guards to prevent the chain from jumping off when the rider is hammering through rocky sections. A loose chain would not only make pedalling impossible, it would also possibly hook up in the wheel, or onto the rider, resulting in a crash.

Disc brakes are the first and obvious choice for the downhill bike. Apart from offering powerful stopping performance, they continue to

work even when the wheel is buckled. But heat generated by a good downhill run can be enough to make the disc turn blue from the excessive heat, giving you a nasty burn should you inadvertently touch it.

Wide handlebars provide the means of control through the rocky sections, allowing the rider to guide the huge knobbly tyres and rims over the smoothest or fastest route.

Most downhill bikes use standard 26-in wheels, but in a wider section to allow a more solid tyre profile. Increasingly, though, smaller diameter 24-in (610-mm) rims are used with huge 3-in (76-mm) tyres, giving a similar overall rolling diameter, but with more cushioning and more grip. The downside, however, is that even more weight is added to the bike.

With all this extra metal and rubber, it is not unusual

for a downhill bike to weigh at least twice that of a good quality cross-country bike. But when you see the speeds at which the top riders descend on tracks that you'd think twice about walking down, you can understand why.

ABOVE: Downhill riders usually have a more substantial physical build than cross-country racers.

LEFT: This downhill bike almost resembles a motorbike.

Dirt Jump/Dual Slalom Bike

As downhilling became increasingly more popular over the last few years, many riders were attracted to the thrills that the downhill provides, but clearly didn't have enough elevation to warrant large amounts of rear-wheel travel. They wanted bikes that are just as much fun as downhill machines, but that would continue to be useful in their local environments. Disused BMX tracks, building sites and purpose-built jumps in wooded areas became the proving ground as lightweight cross-country race trail machines were broken. Enterprising local builders began making frames tough enough to stand the

OPPOSITE TOP LEFT: Tricks and stunts and time in the air is what's important.

OPPOSITE TOP RIGHT: As in trials, dirt jumpers don't use their saddles much!

OPPOSITE BELOW: Dual slalom is another form of mountain biking.

BELOW RIGHT: Make sure your bike fits!

beating, and BMX builders began getting calls for 26-inch-wheeled versions of their dirt-jump framesets. The result? A whole new subculture which used the strong equipment developed for the downhill, but with a tough hardtail frameset that can stand a beating. Riders often ran long-travel forks like a downhill bike and a low seat like a trials bike as well as a single rear brake, like a BMX.

The dirt-jump bike is a design mongrel that's taking mountain biking to new places. Though dirt jumping mostly concentrates on just that – jumping – there is a close crossover in equipment with dual slalom, essentially head-to-head downhill racing on a man-made course, much like a downhill BMX track. Dual slalom isn't the same as dirt jumping, but it's a competitive outlet for riders who are keen to determine 'who is the best'.

Typical dirt jump/dual slalom oversize framesets are made from aluminium, with stress-transfer gussets welded in place to beef up the frame. The front fork is usually a long-travel unit, fitted with either a disc brake, a V brake or no brake at all. Dirt jumpers ride with no front brake to allow

bar-spins and crashes without them getting tangled up in unnecessary cabling. A rear brake is retained to allow stopping (obviously) but also is used to control the position of the bike in the air. Braking the rear wheel pitches the front of the bike downward and can be used to control and correct the flight of the bike once the rider has left the lip of the jump.

Sizing

A good supplier will sell you a bike that fits you correctly, while a bad one is likely to recommend one they probably wish to clear from stock: it is therefore important to know the right way of tackling this problem. For cross-country use, a rider should have at least 4in (10cm) of clearance between the top tube of the bike and the

top of their legs (riding shoes on) when they're standing on the ground, their feet flat on the floor. Any deviation from this and you're more than likely to have a painful collision with the bike should you ever, or rather whenever, you have to leap off the saddle out on the trail. Many riders have far more than 4 inches of clearance, and ride with their

seat posts at full extension. It is the riding position which often dictates the size of bike, as stems, bars and seat posts are all available allowing you to place the bars where you want them. A smaller frame is a lighter frame, and providing the seat post gives enough extension and is correctly positioned in the frame, then there will be no problem with running a lot of seat post extension on a small frame with a high-rise stem and a riser bar. However, smaller-sized bikes will always have shorter top tubes than a larger size, and what the rider will end up with is a frame that's got everything at the right height, but with bars that are too close to the saddle. Fitting a longer-reach stem is an option, but put too much extension on the stem and you'll have too much weight over the front wheel, making steering awkward.

Be guided by a good supplier, pay attention to

sizing (road bikes are far larger for the same-height rider), and try several different bikes to discover which one feels right for you.

Customizing

Although mountain bikes are improving every year, it is unlikely that every off-the-shelf brand will be perfect for every rider. Beginners might not think that they would notice the difference between different components fitted to a bike, but even simple changes such as stem length, bar width, grip type, tyre design or saddle position can make the bike feel totally different. Large tyres run at a low pressure, while a fat padded saddle and swept-back handlebars can make even the sprightliest bike feel like a beach cruiser.

Although there are many different brands of mountain bike, many of the components are interchangeable. However, even though you would never, or even wish to fit a Ford gearbox into a Mercedes, there's no problem with fitting parts from a specialized bike to that of a Fisher or Trek. Many things are standard, which means that there are a stack of parts available at your local bike store waiting to upgrade the performance of your bike.

Even something as simple as a tyre can take many different forms. Different compounds are available, as are tread patterns and cross sections. Practically any mountain bike tyre will fit onto any mountain bike rim, the only exception being the

OPPOSITE TOP: Add things to your bike to improve your comfort – such as a mudguard...

OPPOSITE BELOW: ... or a trailer, which is attached to the rear of the bike and useful for carrying luggage...

BELOW: ... or a complete set of luggage.

very narrowest road-specific slick tyres which will only fit on some of the narrower rims. Ninety-nine per cent of mountain-bike tyres on the market will fit easily onto the same proportion of bike rims on the street.

Handlebars, saddles, grips, chains, and all the associated paraphernalia are all interchangeable to allow you to customize your bike to the way you want it.

If it comes fitted with run-of-the-mill components, you can invest in higher quality parts which will not only last

longer but also function more efficiently throughout their lifetime. They all use the same fixings (braze-ons) on the frame and though some parts must be upgraded as a whole system, they will fit onto most bikes.

Modern V-brake systems must be used with the corresponding compatible brake levers so as to ensure safe operation, and some types of gear shifter must be used with the correct type of rear mech and even cabling. It also goes without saying that you can't run a nine-speed shifter on a bike which has only eight

sprockets on the rear cassette.

You can add an assortment of bits and pieces to the bike too. Riders wishing to carry equipment can bolt on racks and add panniers, or fix attachments to allow trailers to be hauled. Mudguards can be added, lighting systems – the list is endless.

You can add suspension forks, or change the wheelset for a lighter, higher-performance model – it's all possible due to the fact that most bikes have parts designed to be interchangeable with others.

Chapter Two
What Kit?

Although it is quite possible to ride a bike wearing jeans, T-shirt and regular training shoes, you are not likely to be very comfortable in them. Clothing especially designed for mountain biking has in fact developed from a combination of general outdoor clothing and specialist cycle gear resulting in kit that feels good to ride in, is durable in the inevitable crashes that will occur, and stylish enough to avoid people thinking you've escaped from the local fetishist's convention. Over the last few years, Lycra and its cousin Spandex have made it possible to buy modern biking clothing that look much like ordinary outdoor wear, aside from the bike-specific cuts entailed. A cycling pullover or shirt made of fleece may look very similar to one designed for hiking, but look closer and you will notice that the arms are longer, the front is higher, the back is longer and there is a deeper zip at the front. Bike gear works when you're on a bike in the cycling position and it is only when you have experienced a huge gap above your shorts, a shirt bunched up at the front and icy cold

wrists that you'll realize why hiking clothes don't always work as well on a bike as they do off it. So here's a tip: when trying on cycling clothes, assume a cycling position to see what they feel like.

From the point of view of comfort, cycling shorts are the most essential purchase. Though they're often what many would consider to be the worst aspect of bike clothing, you can always hide them under loose-fitting shorts of any description, as their comfort benefits are worth any fashion faux-pas

ABOVE: Clothing can be performance-orientated, fashionable, or both.

LEFT: Bike shorts help keep you comfortable all day long.

OPPOSITE LEFT: A traditional bike helmet, with a peak.

OPPOSITE RIGHT: A full-face helmet for the more extreme, and possibly more dangerous kinds of mountain biking.

that may result. Cycling shorts are fitted with a synthetic leather pad which is worn directly next to the skin, without underwear, and the fact that it is seamless will ensure a chafe-free ride once you have become accustomed to the pedalling action and saddle pressure.

Though you might think it strange to 'go commando' with cycling shorts, adding a layer of underwear would in fact introduce more chafing points, with layers of fabric forming painful ridges and extra seams to dig into the skin. Of course, if you are a regular cyclist, it pays to have several pairs of cycling shorts so that you can alternate them. Don't wear them more than once without washing

them, and turn them inside out before hanging them to dry outside so that the sun's ultra-violet rays can do their work in disinfecting them.

A helmet is another essential and, depending on where you live in the world, could well be a legality too. The topic of helmet wearing is a controversial one and there are many different points of view, one being their mandatory wear. However, there is another school of thought that actually wearing a helmet may tempt riders to take unnecessary risks. Whatever the arguments of the case, the fact remains that head injuries kill, and a great many people (including myself) have had accidents from which we have walked

away due solely to the fact of wearing what to some may be an unpopular item. Accidents come in various forms, some avoidable because they are the result of misplaced confidence, some through component failure; always remember that wearing a helmet increases your chances of survival and going bare-headed is NOT an option.

When looking for a helmet to buy, above all make sure it fits. Small heads, big heads, ponytails and big hair – all are catered for. Price and comfort are no longer reasons to avoid head-protection, as there are many cheap helmets about that offer excellent certified protection, and others that by virtue of their aerodynamics are actually

more comfortable on a bike than going bare headed.

Helmets for mountain biking are usually peaked, which probably started out as a fashion feature but has ended up making complete sense. In hot, dry climates, peaks are great for keeping the sun and bugs out of your eyes, while in wetter climes they are good protection from rain and mud. Whatever: a peak on your helmet sets you up clearly as a mountain biker. You may be mocked without one, and you will definitely feel more like one of the crowd if you wear one.

Downhill riders use motocross-style full-face helmets, giving them extra protection at the higher speeds at which they're riding. The helmets are either true MX-issue models (albeit the more expensive and hence lighter models around) or bicycle-modified MX-designed with extra ventilation and perhaps giving better visibility. Riders interested in trials and dirt-jumping have started to adopt the 'skate'-style helmet used by BMX riders and rollerbladers. Whatever the case, it's interesting to note that helmets are now regarded as 'cool'.

The final items in our list of essentials are gloves. When you are a beginner, it is inevitable that you will crash – often. Traditional cycling gloves have always been short-fingered with leather palms and knitted cotton backs. Downhill mountain biking brought motocross elements to the sport, and with it fully-fingered armoured motocross gloves. Manufacturers have put these designs on a diet and the result is the full-finger mountain-bike glove. These are noticeably different from a full MX article thanks to their lack of knuckle protection which isn't needed as mountain bikers don't usually have to contend with the company of 40 other riders who are throwing rocks up from their rear wheels. A good mountain-bike glove has fingers, a secure wrist closure, some sort of padding for the heel of the hand, a tough leather (or synthetic) palm, not forgetting a terry-towelling patch (and this is a climate

thing too) to either wipe your forehead, or wipe your nose, depending on how hot or cold it is.

Extra Kit
There are many different types of shoe on the market to cater for the wide variety of people taking to mountain bikes. Some are little more than road-race shoes with extra tread on the soles, and at the other extreme there are those that look for all the world like regular training shoes but which have hidden within them a stiffened sole and bolt-in points for mounting to pedals.

Racing and high-performance bikes have popularized the 'clipless' pedal, which is a system in two parts. A hardened metal cleat bolts to the sole of the shoe, which can be engaged into a clipping system on the pedal body. The shoes can be released from the pedals by rotating the ankles outwards but, aside from this movement, the shoes (and so the feet) are mounted to the pedals with a small amount of rotational and lateral movement. This gives a very secure pedalling position and ensures that the foot stays in position when riding on rocky tracks, where a flat pedal (the shoe simply resting on the pedal body) might very well slip.

However, for extremes of use, such as downhilling and stunt riding, many riders prefer to use an aggressively

profiled pedal which has sharp teeth that dig into the rider's shoes – it's a matter of horses for courses. Many novice riders find the sensation of being 'locked' to their bikes rather disconcerting, but once they have become accustomed to it find it a secure way, not only of allowing them to pedal more efficiently, but also to maintain control of the bike more fully. You cannot be in full control if your feet are flapping around looking for the pedals!

Rain and other inclement weather conditions are always a problem. The complete mountain biker's wardrobe would ideally have a shell jacket for every occasion, but for practical purposes some compromise has to be made. Lightweight wind- and shower-proof jackets made of fabrics such as Pertex are able to repel short bursts of heavy rain, protect against wind chill and 'breathe' in order to keep the rider cool and comfortable when they're working hard. Better quality fabrics, such as Gore-Tex, offer increased protection against heavy rain, but there is an ultimate trade-off between breathability, full protection and 'feel'. Get yourself a bomb-proof jacket that's breathable and waterproof and you may well have something that feels like a suit of armour. Several companies are now using a stretchable Gore-Tex, but as

you would expect of a fabric that's stretchable, yet retains its breathability and waterproof characteristics (no mean feat), this is a very expensive option.

As you continue to ride your bike you'll become aware of other items that may be useful. Many cyclists develop extensive summer, winter and spring wardrobes, along with specialist gloves, neck warmers, thermal underwear, sleeveless vests, breathable waterproof helmet covers and the like. It's all there in the stores, tempting you to part with your cash, and we haven't even discussed the subject of heavily logo'd riding kit!

Other Kit

There are items other than clothing that are well worth the investment in making your riding more enjoyable. There are drinks systems which fit onto your back like a rucksack but hold a water bladder from which you can drink via a hosepipe acting like a straw. A simple valve on the end of the tube prevents water from running out. They have an advantage over the simple water bottle as they aren't in the direct path of spray from the front wheel – so you shouldn't get a mouthful of mud when you are expecting a refreshing drink. Good drinking systems also have extra rucksack-like pockets in which to carry spares and tools. They are

ideal for mountain biking and are well worth the initial investment.

Sports 'glasses' differ from conventional 'street' sunglasses in that their lenses are always made of high-impact plastic rather than glass. They're designed to fit close to the face and are available in a huge variety of tints. Many mountain bikers use clear glasses all year round to protect their eyes from grit and flying insects. Amber lenses are also popular for dark days as their tint tends to exaggerate colours and shadows, giving better vision on hazy days.

Seatpacks that strap under the saddle are ideal places to store tools and spares you may need on a ride. Later on,

OPPOSITE ABOVE: Cycling shoes have tough uppers and stiff soles to transfer power efficiently.

OPPOSITE BELOW: Winter cycling clothing, including yellow waterproof jacket, helmet, glasses and gloves.

BELOW: A rucksack-like drinking system allows you refreshment while riding.

RIGHT: Getting away from it all with just the bare essentials.

BELOW: The car rack is a great accessory for those who prefer to ride their bikes further from home.

we will be covering what tools you should take out on a ride to ensure you get back in one piece should problems occur.

Specialist mountain bikers may use equipment that's quite different from that of run-of-the-mill bikers. Downhill racers use body armour straight from the pitlane of motorcycle racing. Made from close-fitting padding with plastic, this will protect against most high speed, high impact crashes, but aren't a life insurance certificate: bones can still be broken.

Bike Racks

Suitable areas where they can mountain bike and which are accessible just beyond their own front doors are available only to the lucky few. For the majority, however, part of mountain biking involves getting themselves and their bikes to the trailhead. Actually riding your bike the full distance on tarmac is of course possible, but if you wish to transport your bike by car, what are the available options?

Fortunately, even small hatchbacks have boots or trunks large enough to take a couple of bikes with the wheels removed; but the extra trouble and mess involved is enough to deter all but the most determined souls.

Car racks are available on which you can strap your bike and come in three basic types: mounted on the roof, the trunk or hatchback, or onto a tow-bar-mounted rack. Tow-bar-mounted racks are generally the most secure, and also avoid possible damage to paintwork that the makers of

'strap-on' racks always promise won't happen, but invariably does. Roof-rack mounting is a good option for smaller cars, and for people who don't wish to have a tow-bar fitted and want immediate access to the boot or trunk.

When mounting a bike rack to the rear of the car, take care to ensure that the number plates and lights, if obstructed, are displayed on a lighting board fixed to the bike. And finally, make sure your bike is well secured. Bikes have been known to survive falls at high speeds from cars, but the damage caused to them or to other road users is something best avoided.

Travel Kit

If you're intending to travel abroad with your bike, you'll need to discuss with your travel agent or airline how your bike can best be accommodated. There are a variety of ways of packing a bike for travel, with varying amounts of preparatory work. I've known people ride a bike

ABOVE: You can still be happy and comfortable while carrying all you need.

OPPOSITE: Even your youngest child can come along, but make sure that he is well strapped in, is wearing a protective helmet and is dressed appropriately for the season.

to the airport and simply push their bike to the check-in desk, affix a label and send it off as it is. At the other end of the scale, however, are the types who strip their bikes down and pack the pieces into specially protected padded flight cases.

Bike bags are a good option for most people. These are large and padded with special compartments for wheels, saddle and pedals and have a tough enough lining and various fixings to protect the bike in transit. Spacers should be fitted to the open ends of the frame (where the wheels would fit) to avoid any possible crush damage during transit. There's nothing worse than travelling for hours or even days to the perfect riding location only to find that your bike is too damaged to ride.

Carrying Kit

Whether you are intending to bring home the shopping, or carry a tent and sleeping gear over rough ground, you'll need the right equipment to enable you to carry them on your bike.

Traditional bikes use traditional equipment – usually a rack and panniers, a saddlebag or handlebar bag. These can work on mountain bikes providing that the terrain you may encounter isn't too extreme. Many mountain bikes have fittings for attaching such racks, though they're more common

at the lower end of the market. (For some reason, manufacturers seem to think that people who have more money to spend want race-replica bikes.) Universal fittings are available to attach racks and other carrying gadgets to your bike, even if the manufacturer hasn't already supplied them.

Most mountain bikers don't carry equipment on the bike, preferring a backpack which often doubles as a drinking system (mentioned above). These have the advantage that they move with you, rather than remaining as a dead weight

on the bike, and keep the bike feeling lively even when carrying moderate amounts of weight. The problem of course is that the weight is carried on the body, and puts extra stress and strain on the rider. It's not just the shoulders that ache either – that extra weight going through the saddle will also cause an aching back and saddle soreness too. Probably a comfortable limit for a fit rider to carry on their backs is 15lb (6.8kg), but even that is going to be felt when travelling over tough terrain. Carefully packed, this will be enough weight to include a

tent, sleeping bag and small stove for an overnight trip.

Should you wish to carry more weight, then panniers which fit over a rack are probably what you need. Make sure that if you're riding in rough terrain, the panniers have suitably tough fixings to secure them to the rack firmly. Many have been designed for road use, where they're unlikely to be subjected either to the high loads or to the vibration that an off-road tour would put them to. They should fasten securely to the rack, rather than clipping over the top, and be held in place by an

ABOVE: 'You're not pedalling!' Trailer bikes are a safer option when cycling with children on busy roads.

OPPOSITE: Trailers can be used to carry either luggage or children.

sure no control cables are fouled or snagged during fixing, as the steering moves from side to side – no mean feat if you're going for this option. It does have the advantage, however, that the sleeping bag is held securely, and even forms a rudimentary 'fairing' to smooth your aerodynamic path along the trail. You can also see when it's about to fall off too!

Kids

Children and bikes go well together. Of course, their strength and stamina isn't as developed as adult riders, but with care, preparation and common sense they can be encouraged to enjoy biking as much as anyone else, and still allow their adult companions a good fun ride.

For very small children, the options are between a secure bike trailer and a child seat. Some bike trailers have a provision to take a child's car seat, which means that even the youngest child can be carried safely. Car seats can only be used when the child can sit up, usually around nine months. However, use your common sense when it comes to the terrain you're contemplating. Pediatricians warn of the dangers of subjecting children to hard jarring until even the age of four or five, as their brains are not mature enough to withstand the knocks caused by the sort of repeated buffeting they could be subjected to in a trailer on a

elasticated strap. Beware: if you can pull them off easily you can be sure they'll leap off your rack at the most inconvenient moment.

Large packs which fit under the saddle are useful for a variety of things, not the

least toolkits. They fit neatly in with the lines of the bike, important not only for fashion reasons, but also so that they don't hinder you while you're riding the bike.

Some off-road tourists utilize the space beneath their

handlebars and secure lightweight items there. Objects placed high on the bike should be as light as possible: consequently bulky, but not unduly heavy items, such as sleeping bags, are ideally positioned here. Make

rough track. It really is common sense to judge the speed and severity of any ride and to make a decision accordingly.

As children grow older they will eventually learn to ride their own bikes, but these will probably be unsuitable for extended rides with an adult on even gentle off-road terrain. Unless the adult is willing to cut short their own ride, or to spend much of the ride pushing the child while pedalling (which is dangerous for all involved), then the best answer is a trailer bike. This is a specialist bike that attaches to the seat post or specially made rack on the back of an adult bike. A set of cranks drive the rear wheel, and the result is that the child can pedal as much as they like

and freewheel when they feel they've had enough.

As the child won't be pedalling as much as the adult and, in the case of the child in the child seat, won't be pedalling at all, remember, if conditions warrant, to dress them up warmly. They'll need a couple of extra layers compared to the cyclist who'll be producing heat through exercise in the usual way. Ending up with a cold child miles from home isn't much fun – I've had to surrender my socks for them to use as gloves on a couple of occasions!

Toolkits for Trail Use

Your bike will break down on the trail. It's inevitable. Plan for such an occurrence rather than hoping it will never happen, and you'll always get

home without too much of a problem. Of course, there is little use having the tools if you don't know what to do with them, so make sure you study the section on maintenance (page 50) and get an experienced cyclist to show you a few simple repairs. If you understand how your bike works, you are more likely to be able to get it going again in the event of a breakdown. Bikes aren't complicated things and with a little knowledge, the right tools and a modicum of common sense you should be able to fix most problems that occur on the trail.

As has already been mentioned, you would be well advised to keep your bike well maintained at all times. Small irksome

problems that can be spotted and fixed at home can, if left, become large problems that prevent a bike from functioning as it should. Nowhere else is the proverb 'A stitch in time saves nine' more apt, and you'll save wear and tear on other components as well.

There is one breakdown, however, that you can't protect against. Or can you? Punctures have been the bane of the cyclist's life since the pneumatic tyre was invented, and they're pretty much a fact of life for us all. However, many punctures are avoidable. Running tyres too soft can cause them to impact puncture on rocks or sharp edges, and the inner tube will be trapped between the tyre wall and the rim, resulting in

LEFT: Carry a complete toolbox with you or, failing this, a multi-tool.

OPPOSITE: There is no other way you can pump up a tyre if you haven't got a pump– so always carry one, together with a spare tube and puncture kit.

a double-holed 'snake bite' flat. In this case, checking your tyre pressure, and even riding in such a way as to avoid hazardous terrain, can protect you from punctures. There are other examples: incorrectly fitting tyres, brakes rubbing the sidewalls of the tyre, allowing the valves of the inner tube to get dirty – they'll all result in punctures which will cause untold heartache when you're out on the trail. Unless you've the kit to fix them – a pump, spare tube or puncture kit – you'll be facing a long push home.

The types of tools you will need to keep your bike in good order while out on the trail depend upon what components your bike has on it, how well maintained it is, and how long you'll be off

riding it. However, as a rough guide, shown below are the bare minimum. The easier way to take many of these items is in the form of a multi-tool. These are available from many different

manufacturers, though it's worth noting that you generally get what you pay for. Practise in advance using the tool so that you know what to do when you really need it. Does that 6-mm hex

key actually allow you to tighten your stem or seat post correctly? Will the chain tool work? There's no point just hoping that it will be alright on the night – make absolutely sure that it is!

2.5, 4, 5, 6, 8mm hex
 keys (to suit
 components)
2 tyre levers
1 puncture kit (patches, glue,
 chalk)
1 spare tube
Pump
Chain tool

*In addition, these items
can be extremely useful:*
1 small crosshead
 screwdriver
Spoke key (if you
 know how to use it)
A small bottle of oil
Zip ties

Chapter Three
How to Ride

To get the best out of them, mountain bikes, when ridden in terrain that is appropriate, require certain techniques. Traction is often limited and the undulations, changing conditions and other trail problems mean that making progress isn't just a matter of turning the pedals round: you need to know how to handle your bike to make it perform properly on tough trails. You'll pick up a lot of these skills as you start riding, and watching advanced riders overtaking you as you stumble is enough to drive you to try harder and practise more frequently. These techniques will come: not all are natural, but they can be learned. Have them in your armoury, ready to use at any time, and you're certain to become a great all-round mountain biker.

The Riding Position

You can't ride a mountain bike if you're not comfortable. If you've got your bike set up correctly, then you should be aiming for a riding position where your elbows are relaxed, bent at about 90 degrees (see above). Hold the handlebar grips firmly, but if you see white knuckles, then you're gripping too tight. Your back should be straight, at about 45 degrees to the ground. Look up, look where you're going, and smile. And relax ... this is meant to be fun!

Stopping

Before you learn how to go fast, you should learn to stop. While riding on a well surfaced road, you can brake practically as hard as you like.

The harder you brake the more abruptly you will stop, and providing you don't go shooting over the handlebars (a possibility) there's the chance that you'll leave large skid marks all over the road.

Off-road, it's different – nothing is as uncertain as braking on an off-road track. Because of the nature of the surface, traction (which is what makes for good braking) can vary from tarmac-like grip to slick-ice in a matter of feet. Braking from riding speed down to a stop will take you across different areas of grip, and the bike will react differently on all of them. Brake hard enough to slow quickly on firm ground and the bike will slip and slide on stickier terrain.

Being a competent off-road rider means learning how to use your brakes: judge the ground you're covering and be aware of what the bike is doing so that you are in a position to prevent a crash. Locking up the front wheel of the bike will cause you to tip over the front on hard ground, but on slippery ground will cause the front wheel to 'wash out' and slide away from you, causing loss of control and a crash. Locking up the rear wheel won't just cause big environmentally damaging skid marks, it will actually make you accelerate as the sliding wheel slows you down less than a well-braked wheel. It will also make the bike harder to control as, now it's sliding, it will be just as happy to slip sideways as it is to go in a straight line.

To remedy this, you've got

OPPOSITE: The correct riding position.

BELOW: Even when it all goes wrong, there's a right way out of the problem.

to learn to brake properly. Find a patch of slightly downhill track and approach it at a middling speed – pedalling, keeping your speed going, but not accelerating. Don't go mad. At a given point (note where), start to brake. Squeeze the levers, both of them, and bring the bike to a halt. Then repeat, trying with the front brake alone, the back brake alone and then both brakes again.

You'll notice very quickly that the front brake allows you to stop a lot quicker than the rear one. You may have learnt from days of riding bikes on tarmac that pulling hard on the front brake causes you to 'endo' over the handlebars and crash. While it's true that if you are heavy-handed and haul the levers on, then you will crash over the bars, used properly, the front brake is far more use than the rear.

Once you've got the hang of what's going on, tentatively try and over-brake (locking a wheel, then releasing it). Feel what the bike does as it begins to slide. By learning what, how and where these things occur you can plan for them happening and when they do be better prepared. Result? Better braking, faster braking and yourself in greater control of your bike.

Climbing

Mountains unfortunately go up, and many beginners consider climbing to be the worst aspect of riding. But in time they'll learn to love it. The challenge of a tough climb, especially a technically steep climb, is something many mountain bikers thought they would never understand but now find addictive.

Being good at climbing takes more than just fitness. One of the world's best mountain-bike racers and climbing expert, Tim Gould, always says 'Start easy, finish hard'. In other words, start a climb in the very lowest gear you have, and shift up as you get comfortable. That way you can gauge your fitness and the severity of the slope, rather than committing yourself to trying to stomp up a 2/3-mile (1-km), 20 per cent grade in 36/28.

Long climbs, particularly at high altitude, are when an extremely low gear will come in very useful. It is possible to select a gear that makes you ride even slower than walking pace, with a technically possible 20/32 bottom gear. For long climbs at altitude, this is something that is well worth examining.

Seated climbing is certainly a lot better for long distance and/or loose conditions. Standing up is good for hammering up a short steep section with good traction, but will wear you out fast on longer climbing sections. However, it is good training!

When climbing sitting down, move slightly forward in the saddle. Move your head close to the stem to keep the front wheel from lifting. Don't pull up on the handlebar, but rather pull backward. Keep your body relaxed and shoulders square to the trail, put the bike in a low gear and spin and try not to look towards the top!

When you're standing and powering up a climb, put the bike in a higher gear. You can't spin as fast when you're standing up, but you can apply more power per stroke, so the higher gear will certainly help.

Descending

A whole new sport has developed around downhilling, indeed, that's actually where mountain biking came from – lots of riders getting together to race old paper-boy bikes down a fire road.

So it might be a surprise to you that it's not the most natural thing in the world, but it's certainly an area where real rider skill can be shown off – unless a rider is truly foolhardy and actually out of control!

When approaching a steep downhill, get yourself settled on the bike, keeping your pedals level (3 and 9 o'clock) and, as the hill drops away, move your weight back. The steeper it is, the more you should move your weight. It is probable that if you're riding down a steep enough hill, you'll be almost sitting on your back tyre.

Slowing down should be done using both brakes, but as long as you have sufficient control, then concentrate on using the front brake. As you've got most of your weight on your front wheel, the front brake has a far greater effect on your rate of descent. When the hills get steep, it doesn't take much for your rear wheel to lock, not only causing large terrain-damaging skid marks, but also making your bike slide from side to side more easily.

As you get used to riding downhill, you can more easily concern yourself with the added problems: don't ride down in the smallest chainring as the chain is liable to flop around. Instead shift to the middle or largest chainring where the tension of the rear mech and the greater number of teeth can keep the chain from dropping off the chainrings. Full-on downhill bikes have a single chainring with an added chain-guide system to keep the chain securely in place, but for general cross-country use, mountain bikes have a built in chainguide – the front mech. If the chain does drop off, often a simple pedal will drag it back on again, though in the worst case a flapping chain can get caught up in your rear tyre tread and bring you to a grinding halt.

Downhilling is where speeds really increase, and due care should be taken. Small trail obstacles that are no problem at lower speeds can cause the bike to begin skipping about and wobbling from side to side. This doesn't

OPPOSITE LEFT: Powering up a climb needs weight to the front of the bike too.

OPPOSITE RIGHT: Downhilling over rocky terrain at speed requires strength, agility and technique.

RIGHT: Take care while negotiating loose rocks.

mean that you should approach every downhill with fear and trepidation; just be aware enough to ride within your limits.

If you greatly enjoy the thrill of high-speed downhill riding, then investigate the sport of downhill racing. Here you can enjoy the thrill of defying gravity in a closed-course situation, without the risk of conflict with any other trail users, the only danger being damage to yourself.

Trails can be used by· many different trail-users, other than bikers, from ramblers and walkers to horse riders and even vehicles. Care

should of course be taken on blind bends and when overtaking other trail users. Inappropriate behaviour only leads to tensions between user groups and can result in trails being closed to bikers. It is therefore in everyone's interest to ride sensibly, particularly at the higher speeds of which mountain bikes are capable.

Cornering

When you are riding a bike, you must strive to be in control from a purely physical point of view. Riding along, the corrections you're making are preventing you from falling over. Though you might think

that in order to turn to the left you pull on the left handlebar, this is not the case.

In fact, to turn to the left, you don't even push on the right handlebar (which would, I suppose be the opposite of pulling on the left). In fact, what you'll find you're doing is pushing on the left handlebar instead. How can it be that pushing on the handlebar makes you go that way? Simple: when you first push on the handlebar, you make the bike swerve (ever so slightly) to the right. Because the momentum of the bike and your body want you to carry straight on, your body begins

to fall to the left. Then, you control that fall to the left by pushing on the left handlebar, steering out of the fall but in actual fact cornering to the left. This is certainly bizarre when you read it, so a better idea is to actually try the manoeuvre on the bike and experience it for yourself.

If you're not doing this – if you're still steering a bike by tugging on' the handlebar on the side of the bike in the direction that you want to go, then you're doing it wrong. Steering by moving the bars isn't a good way to handle a bike once you're above walking pace. Once speeds increase, you should steer the bike by leaning it, controlling the fall by the 'countersteering' methods described above. It might feel strange and unnatural, but the easiest way to practise is to ride with your hands just resting on the grips so that you can only push on the bars, not pull. This provides a far more controlled steering method, and one that works much better when the track you're riding on is rough or slippery.

Wheelies

This most basic of schoolyard tricks can be your best friend when you're learning to ride on real off-road tracks. While riding for miles on one wheel isn't appropriate here, being able to lift the front wheel over obstacles and shift your weight from the front to the rear of the bike is essential. Mountain

LEFT: Rather more than a mere stunt, the wheelie is your friend in need!

BELOW: Likewise, lifting the rear wheel can help you too.

OPPOSITE: Sliding the back wheel helps you to reposition the bike, but may cause erosion to the trail.

biking is a dynamic sport, and the ability to hop the front wheel over rocks or a log is the difference between getting down a track in one piece and either having to stop and stumble, or simply crashing at every obstacle. Whether you execute your wheelie by simply pulling back on the bars, or by pushing hard on the pedals, the result is the same – the front wheel can be lifted clear of the ground. Practise popping the front wheel up on kerb-stones or small obstacles on the road before putting these manoeuvres into practice on the trail. And be prepared to apply speed and effort to these obstacles. Go too slow and your rear wheel may stop dead as it hits its target. Going too fast, however, and getting the

timing wrong, will land you in serious trouble. So take care.

Once you've perfected the standard wheelie so that with care you can lift the front wheel off the ground whether you're coasting along or pedalling hard, you can move on to more advanced techniques, such as the wheelie-pivot. Here the skilled rider can lift the front wheel off the ground, using their hips to swivel the bike round to move the front wheel one way or the other. It's a useful technique on tricky climbs, allowing you to reposition the front wheel on a more suitable trajectory. Combine this with a rear-wheel lift (see below) and you will find you are able to move smoothly up a rocky climb that would otherwise be impossible.

opposite direction to the corner, giving 'opposite lock' steering control.

To a beginner, riding like this would seem like asking to fall off. Sliding the tyres sideways can't be a good idea? Can it? Drifting around corners isn't anything you'd set out to do, but you can practise it. However, it's a high-speed technique and if you tackle it slowly it simply won't work. The tyres can't slide unless you are exerting enough force on them, and that doesn't happen until speed and technique increase to such a level that these things can occur. The only time you may find your tyres sliding sideways is on off-camber turns, where there's not enough ground to support the tyre properly. In these situations, a slip will probably cause you to put a foot down or possibly you'll crash. Once you're up to speed controlling sliding-tyre situations, then you'll be far better able to cope with them.

Practise by cornering on damp ground; then you'll get the true feel of what is happening as the bike begins to slide. Stop the slide by adjusting your weight fore-and-aft or, in the worst case, using a foot to stop the slide.

The Rear-Wheel Lift

If nothing else, the ability to lift the front and rear wheels will teach you much about weight distribution and the effect it has on a bike. Though with practice you should be able to lift either the front wheel (by executing a wheelie) or the rear wheel (by quickly shifting your weight forward), riding really starts to become fluent when you combine these techniques and use them dynamically as you're going along. Combine these with the

advanced braking skills and the cornering techniques you are learning and you'll end up in situations where you're using all the techniques we've described so far, including braking in a corner and shifting your weight to correct tyre slide.

Drifting

Cornering at high speeds on tracks with loose surfaces can produce interesting results. Depending on weight distribution, tyre type and

riding style, either the front or rear of the bike can break away. Either will result in the bike changing line from the one it was holding with the tyres gripping. With the front end sliding, the bike will tend to understeer, going straight on in a corner, and with the rear end slipping the bike will oversteer, requiring less turning of the handlebars to get it to corner successfully. Indeed, when the rear wheel is sliding, the handlebars often need to be turned in the

Bunnyhopping

The ability to lift your bike clear of the ground comes into its own when riding fast on trails where obstacles are in the way, or for showing off in

Not for jumping over rabbits, the bunnyhop helps you clear obstacles along the trail.

the car park before the ride has started. A bunnyhop is the name of the technique used to lift both wheels simultaneously clear of the ground. When it's used as you're riding along, it enables you to clear obstacles that might otherwise cause a crash or at least cause you to slow right down. Sharp-edged rocks or roots, or even kerb-stones can be easily cleared. Two techniques exist: the classic bunnyhop technique involves first wheelieing the bike, then shifting your weight forward as you would for a rear-wheel lift. Movements should be fluid while springing upwards, allowing the bike to come up underneath you. The other technique, made possible largely by the invention of clipless pedals is simply a matter of crouching down and springing upwards, pulling the bike up with your feet which are securely fastened to the pedals. Purists prefer the first technique, but most experienced riders use a combination of the two, and the second 'pull it up' technique is certainly easier to learn.

This is the first 'trick' move that many riders learn, and it can be seen, as described, to be simply an evolution of the wheelie and the rear-wheel lift executed in one move. Some of the tricks that follow aren't so simple and few have any actual trail value. However, all are tremendous fun.

The Switzerland Squeaker

Who makes up these names? Maybe it's because someone in Switzerland first managed to do it and his shoes squeaked on the tyre in the process. Who knows?

The trick involves riding the bike backwards, on the front wheel, using your feet to turn the front wheel. It's rather amazing to watch but can have very painful consequences if it all goes wrong, leaving the rider plummeting to earth head first. This has even been performed on a tandem with only one rider on board.

Standing up, the rider proceeds to ride, then abruptly pulls on the front brake. The bike goes into an 'endo' (where it rocks forward on its front wheel), at which point the rider removes his feet from the pedals and places them on the front tyre behind the fork crown. Then, by releasing the front brake and walking on the tyre, the bike can be made to go backwards. When the rider has had enough, he releases the front brake, drops the back wheel back onto the ground and rides off.

The No-Footed Endo

An endo is a trick where you rock the bike on the front wheel, holding the balance point for as long as possible. A no-footed endo is the same, but without placing the feet on the pedals. It's also quite different, for when you've got the bike in the air, removing your feet from the pedals tends to make the bike shoot forward more sharply. You've got to counteract this by sitting on the saddle hard when the bike's coming up off the ground. In other words, it's a balancing act where good leg extension earns brownie points. Pointing the toes is cool too.

OPPOSITE: The Switzerland Squeaker.

BELOW: The No-Footed Endo.

OPPOSITE: The Seat-Stand Wheelie.

LEFT: The Statue of Liberty.

The Seat-Stand Wheelie

Standard wheelies are hard enough, but here's a trick that's straight out of the circus. Proceed to ride along putting one foot on the seat while leaving the other flapping around for balance. Now haul backwards and do a wheelie. This is incredibly difficult because of the high centre of gravity; the seat-stand wheelie has a tendency to accelerate at the vital moment, so you've got to keep everything together to avoid just shooting the bike off forward as you pull up. This hurts when it goes wrong.

The Statue of Liberty

This is trials rider Hans Rey's trademark flatland trick. Basically, by various means (wheelie, backhops, etc.), he gets the bike vertical, then balances on it straddling the bike. This is a remarkable manoeuvre, but if you can't work out how it's done, don't even try.

49

Chapter Four
Maintenance

Maintaining your bike yourself isn't just a good way of saving money, it means that in the event of your bike breaking down far from a friendly repair shop you'll be better able to deal with the problem. Bikes are simple structures, and it is usually possible to figure out for yourself what has gone wrong. Certainly, some parts can be considered potentially dangerous to work on yourself; setting brakes incorrectly could well cause a crash. But with a little care and diligence, the correct mechanical techniques can be learned which will make your bike work that much better. If you develop the necessary skills to enable you to look after your bike yourself, then it is likely to be always in better condition than if you resorted to infrequent professional (and expensive) help in times of crisis.

To carry out basic repairs and maintenance, you'll need a basic repair kit. As bikes have developed, happily, manufacturers have paid more attention to the requirements of the home mechanic. It's in bike manufacturers' interests that parts should slot together quickly; that way they can fit

ABOVE: Fixing a puncture isn't usually anything to smile about.

RIGHT: This is reason enough for giving your bike a good clean.

certainly not cheap. Normal car shampoo is the best bet. Washing up liquid and other detergents can be used, but aficionados of cycle cleaning (there are some, they're the ones toothbrushing under their saddles!) claim that only car shampoos have the low salt content that will avoid corrosion. It makes sense, but so long as you wash the thing with plenty of water, any detergent is better than none.

LEFT: Cleaners and oils are available from your dealer to help you keep your bike in good condition.

BELOW: If you can, thoroughly clean your bike after every ride, but if time is short, at least clean the drive train.

more bikes onto the production line. These quick-fit tricks mean that for the home mechanic complex tools are pretty much a thing of the past as bikes can now be serviced with a handful of hex keys and a couple of spanners.

Oils and greases might look the same, whatever the application, but the loadings on a bike are different to those of a car engine. Lubricants made specifically for bicycles work better: the heavy grease used in car axles is often too thick to work well on bike bearings though engine oil will work on a bike chain but is extremely messy. Likewise, all-purpose sprays that can cure squeaking door hinges are sometimes useful in the bike workshop, but a proper bike chain lube is better still. Remember that getting the right toolkit is the ultimate step in the right direction.

Cleaning

There are several approaches to cleaning bikes. The first and simplest is not to clean the

bike at all. Proponents of this method boast of how much more riding time they manage to get in, and that cleaning a bike doesn't make it work any better. Up to a point they're right. Buffing a frame to a high gloss and cleaning the underside of your saddle with a toothbrush won't make the bike go faster, further or allow you to have more fun. But keeping the moving parts and bearing units of your bike free from grime will prolong the life of the components, and make them function more efficiently when they are working.

The very minimum cleaning you should do after a ride (every ride where a bike gets dirty) is to clean off the drive train. Many brands of specialist degreasing agents are available to speed up this task. If you're using one, make sure it's a bike-specific one that won't attack the rubber of your tyres or the aluminium surfaces of the components on your bike. Used correctly they're good, but they are

Scrub the chain, sprockets, chainrings and mechs with a stiff-bristled brush. Hot water and detergent will lift the accumulated grime on the gears, though there shouldn't be too much to clean because you're meant to be doing this every ride.

Release the brake cables from the brakes and scrub the brakeblocks and tyre sidewalls. Mud build-up here can rub through the tyres and cause damage: you'll hear the rubbing but you may not know what the noise is until it's too late. Clean regularly and inspect for damage as this is easier than having a split

tyre miles from anywhere.

Hose the bike down with a regular low-pressure hosepipe, or simply pour water over the frame. Jet-wash-type systems can be used to clean bikes but in the wrong hands are an ideal way of blasting all the grease out of the bearings, replacing it with water instead, which is far from ideal.

Let the bike stand for a few minutes, then get out the water-displacing light lubricant. This is the stuff for fixing squeaky hinges, and it is ideal for spraying over the bike to drive the moisture out of the chain and pivots. Attack the bike with the

spray, but take care to avoid the rim and brake surfaces. Proceed gently, then spray the chain while spinning the cranks backwards, squirting the rear mech while shielding the rim from overspray. Squirt the pedals, the brake lever pivots and you can even give the frame a once over.

Then, if possible, leave the bike next to a warm radiator or in a warm room to dry off as it it is astonishing how quickly rust can develop. Rust can envelop a chain overnight, and while it is largely superficial, left to happen time and again will do nothing for the life of your chain.

ABOVE: Oil the chain to drive off moisture after washing.

OPPOSITE LEFT: Get oil onto the rear sprockets too.

OPPOSITE RIGHT: Cables can rust – oil them, but keep the oil off the brake pads.

After an hour or so, go back to the bike and oil the chain. It's best to do it now as the lube will have had a chance to 'set up' and work into the chain. The result? A clean bike, ready to ride next time. Just check the tyre pressure and go.

While cleaning your bike, it's a good idea to check for any damage. Are there any knobs missing on the tyres? Dents or cracks appearing in the paint aren't there because of old age. Something has been bumped or bent. Why? When? Have any bolts dropped out? Checking these things over is a part of being a good mechanic. However, if

there is anything you're not sure about, consult a professional.

Cracks form on bikes because they're being stressed past their limit, or because of fatigue failure due to poor design or faults in manufacturing. Or it may be a freakish occurrence. If cracks occur, they do so in the areas of highest stress which, on a bike, are on the undersides of the headtube/downtube joint or right at the back of the forks, which is where all the weight goes when the bike is pounding over the trail. It can usually stand it, but in certain circumstances, such

as when you've T-boned a rock or disappeared into a ditch with your full weight on the bike, things can get bent. In the old days, of course, forks would just bend, but present-day suspension forks are far stronger than the frame in frontal impact. Indeed forks are so strong that, in a crash, some 'dual-crown' models have been known to tear the headtube straight off the bike. This you would notice for sure, but after a serious collision it's wise to check that the frame (and forks) are in proper working order. You'll surely notice a big bend because your bike just

won't look right. Once again, if you're unsure, check with your local repair shop.

Chain Wear

Just as the frame has its areas where stress occurs, the bike chain is also destined to have a tortuous and highly stressed life. Pounded by vicious cogs, poorly lubricated, subjected to all manner of mud and muck, and shoved from side to side by the somewhat archaic derallieur system, it's a wonder they work at all. When chains wear they appear to stretch. And it's true. Measure a new chain alongside an old one and

chain at this stage, as the chainrings and sprockets have worn to fit the chain. Replacing one component without the others in the drive train will cause chain slip. The answer to this is to lubricate your chain regularly, and change it as often as you can afford to do so.

There is much talk of the benefits of various chain types. Shimano chains have had bad reviews from many riders but this is often simply because they've been incorrectly installed. A properly joined Shimano chain (which must be connected with a special joining pin) shifts better than any other chain on the market. Fit a Shimano without the pin and it will fall apart. Fit it right, and you'll have it on until the sprocket teeth wear off and it'll shift all the better.

Gear Adjustment

As mountain bike gears are operated by cables, stretch, wear and damage can affect them. Most often, the cables stretch and this results in your not being able to select the lowest gear at the rear, as the shifter can't pull enough cable through to get the mech onto the sprocket. At the front, cable stretch can cause similar problems with shifting to the large chainring. Adjusting for this cable stretch is just a matter of increasing the tension in the cables, taking the slack out of

the system. There are sometimes two places where this adjustment can be made, either where the cables exit the shifters on the handlebar or, in the case of the rear mech, where the cable enters the rear mech.

Turning either of these anti-clockwise winds them out, increasing tension, taking up the slack and making the gears work correctly again. Add tension until the cable no longer hangs slack when in the highest gear (rear) or lowest (front). Then fine-tune with adjustments out or in to tune the performance across the gear range.

Any cable friction will throw this adjustment out: ensure that the cables are free-running and lubricate them with a light oil (not grease). Release the cables from their cable stops by putting the bike into a low gear (rear) and high gear (front) and then, without pedalling, shifting to the opposite (high – front, low – rear). This will loosen the cables and allow the cable outers to be pulled from the cable stops. Then the outers can be slid to a free section of cable and the cables lubricated with lighweight oil, allowing freer running. The last section of cable for the rear mech, where it loops around from the frame to the mech, is particularly susceptible to water ingress, as the water happily runs down the cable and collects in the cable outer. If left, this

without a doubt the old chain will be longer, not by very much, but definitely longer. This is called 'chain stretch' but it's not caused by the metal of the chain stretching, but by the pivots in the chain wearing. A tiny amount of wear in all the

pivots adds up to a significant amount across the chain. This wear means that the load from the drive train isn't spread across as many teeth on the chainrings and sprockets. What makes matters worse is that you can't simply replace the

OPPOSITE ABOVE: Gear cable adjusters.

OPPOSITE BELOW: Some gears have adjustment at the rear mech too.

RIGHT: Check that your brake pads are not rubbing or worn.

BELOW RIGHT: Adjust the brake cable tension with the lever adjusters for a quick fix or fine tune.

can rust and prevent the gears from working properly. Some more expensive bikes have shields and seals on their cables to limit water and ingress of dirt, but all bikes benefit from being lubricated and thoroughly cleaned. If corroded cables are a real problem where you ride (because of muddy and wet conditions), then scaled cables are available, those from Gore and Avid being among the best.

There are other adjustments you can make to your gears. Both the front and rear mechs have adjustment screws which alter the movement of the mechs where they stop at each end of their travel. Many people turn to them to adjust the movement when the problem isn't there at all. Any problems with gear changing are far more likely to have come from incorrect cable tension (due to cable stretch) or cable friction (due to dirt

and grime getting into the cables). Adjusting the end-stop screws can cause the chain to jump off the cassette or chainset, possibly causing an accident. Consider these as 'factory set' items that shouldn't be tampered with.

Brake Check

At the beginning of this chapter we spoke about working on the brakes of your bike, and how this could be potentially dangerous. This doesn't mean that you should ignore the mechanics of your braking system. Ignoring worn pads or cables will lead to calamities one way or another. A good visual inspection and some carefully calculated prodding and wobbling can help you ensure that your brakes are working correctly, though it's not as convincing as simply finding out all of a sudden that you have no brakes at all. No one wants to get themselves into a situation where their brakes have failed, which is why it is so worthwhile keeping a check on the state of the various parts of the braking system.

Brake blocks require the most attention. Because of the way they work, they wear down. Rubbing on the rim stops the bike, but it also erodes braking material from the brake pads. In time – how long depends on how and where you ride – the pads will require replacement. There are too many different

sorts of blocks and brakes to comprehensively discuss replacement techniques here, but your bike should have come with manuals covering the procedure. Given time and application to the task,

it's a simple enough operation, but when you attempt it the first time, make sure there is an experienced mechanic available to check things over to make sure everything is correct.

you've pulled the brake levers nearly to the handlebars (which will happen as the pads wear), then wind out the adjusters on the brake levers (as we did with the gear cables) to take out the slack from the system. Some brake levers also have a lock-nut on the adjuster to lock the adjusted brake into it securely. Brake cables can be lubricated just like gear cables. The 'noodle' on V-brakes is particularly susceptible to filling with grit and grime, but a squirt of oil will usually free it up. The same goes for cables. Release the brake cables from the calipers and pull the outer cable from the cable stops on the frame. A squirt of oil, rubbed backwards and forwards, and they'll soon be running perfectly free again. When you're checking your cables, take care to always replace or have replaced any that are frayed. A brake cable snapping when you pull on it to stop hard is a nasty biking surprise. Don't have it happen to you.

Whatever you do, when you've finished adjusting the brakes, check that everything lines up properly, and that the blocks are securely fastened. If your brake blocks are rubbing on the tyre even a fraction, they can cause them to wear and you'll suffer from a spectacularly sudden puncture, which is usually extremely difficult to fix as it will have damaged the tyre too. If you're not comfortable adjusting the brakes and checking for these problems, then avoid tackling them.

What you can do yourself is adjust and lubricate the brake cables. If you find the brakes are only coming on when

ABOVE: Don't set out on a ride without giving everything a quick check over first.

OPPOSITE: You'll be happier and more confident on your bike knowing it has been well maintained.

Chapter Five
World Biking

Moab, Utah, U.S.A.

The state of Utah is home to a legendary area beloved of mountain bikers. Around the town of Moab lie huge expanses of bare rock which rise and fall dramatically, wind-carved into intricate and dramatic, almost oceanic shapes. The naturally created chasms and pillars have formed into bowls, valleys, ascents and plateaux, all wonderfully smooth and organic in appearance, and which makes for quite the most incredible riding experiences on earth. But alongside these wonders are mining trails, created during the 1950s and 60s as the industry probed the entire area in search of uranium and other minerals, creating a

FAR LEFT and BELOW: Moab, Utah. The distinctive slickrock provides a unique riding experience.

network of roller-coaster trails with sandstone arches and contorted buttes, and passing through lush box canyons, along wild vistas, and across slickrock playgrounds. These old mining routes are more rugged and solitary than anything you will find in the now crowded national parks, at times much more scenic, and certainly more complex and awesome.

The great thing about slickrock riding is that while most mountain biking is a quest for traction, there's traction in abundance when riding at Moab. Riders can carve tight lines and climb ascents where the only limiting factor is their own ability to defy gravity.

People have been riding bikes in Moab for years, but mountain biking has brought better equipment to the area and it has suddenly taken off as a Mecca for the sport. Everything is there in Moab and, as a mountain biker, your first challenge will be to choose a trail appropriate for your own skills and inclinations. The next is finding your way in relative safety. The Moab area has a very dry climate, and the temperature can easily reach more than 100F (38C) in the summer months when it is best to ride in the early morning or evening. In any event, be sure to take plenty of water, preferably in a backpack water-bladder and stay on the trails.

LEFT: A solo rider intent on negotiating the water of a creek. Moab isn't just about slickrock — there's plenty of greenery too.

The Moab desert has a very fragile ecosystem. Pinyon pines, cactus, and the cryptobiotic soils are easily damaged by mountain bikes. Cryptobiotic soil is black and crusty and full of living organisms that take years to recover from damage. This soil is the ecological building block of the desert, so mountain bikers should avoid riding through potholes. These small bodies of water are habitats for miniature tadpoles and fairy and clam shrimp that require clean water to complete their life cycles; they should not be used as a splash-zone in which to cool off.

ABOVE: Colorado boasts some stunning riding, and Durango has some of the best.

OPPOSITE: The singletrack is the finest in the world.

Durango, Colorado, U.S.A.

If there is one place in the world that could be called mountain-bike heaven, Durango must be it. An all-year-round sportsville, Durango first developed around winter skiing, but with a town full of active sporting types, the inhabitants soon took to the sport. It was not long before it became a Mecca for mountain biking, conveniently close to the West Coast yet far enough out to avoid day trippers. The rich and famous among them chose it as a place to settle and soon most of the world's top riders have come to own land in the area, among them John Tomac, Greg Herbold and many others. Consequently, frame and component manufacturers either began to set up facilities there or move their outfits to Durango wholesale.

The reason? The riding is perhaps the best around and is possible up to 12,000ft (3658m), and there are trails that descend half that in a matter of miles. In effect, the terrain around Durango is perfect whatever your riding style.

From technical rocky singletrack and smoother fast singletrack, all are surrounded by beautiful views. Local riders tell of spending hours on the trails and seeing no one, and certainly the riding area is so vast that any traffic that occurs close to the town spreads out just a few miles from the trailhead.

Durango is best ridden in the late spring, as the temperature picks up sharply during high summer. However, as with all winter sports resorts, there can be problems with snow blocking trails right through until the middle of the year.

Durango, Colorado. Altitude may have an effect on your performance when you're up there at 12,000ft (3658m).

Morocco is a popular destination for European riders looking for some winter fun in the sun.

OPPOSITE: The Atlas mountains provide a breathtaking scenic backdrop when riding along the rim of this deep gorge.

BELOW: Mountain tracks exist because they have been gradually developed by the local population for their own use. When using them, treat them with respect.

The Atlas Mountains

Morocco is hardly the first place you would think of visiting with a mountain bike. Its history of political turmoil doesn't exactly entice you there, and it is not overly promoted as a paradise for mountain-bikers. But it is covered by a vast track network, used by the population for both motor transport and more basic means of travel. Only main roads are tarmacked, the rest are simple dirt tracks that get narrower and more rudimentary the further from civilization you get. As a result, the riding is quite superb.

Morocco is a Muslim country and as such you should make yourself aware of the religious and cultural observances practised there and modify your own behaviour accordingly. This is a book about mountain biking rather than a travel guide, but it is recommended that you acquaint yourself with local etiquette before you arrive.

There are organized guided tours, and this certainly makes sense as many of them will support you while you are riding by following on behind with a Land Rover. This sounds like going easy on yourself, but in the heat of the day, when you will need to drink 4 pints (2 litres) of water an hour, and you suddenly burst a rear tyre in the middle of a real desert, this is a wise precaution.

Finding your own destination, armed with your own kit, is an exciting idea, and there's always the chance to explore trails further off the beaten tourist track. However, be cautious at all times.

Morocco offers an opportunity to step back in time and see how people live in a very different society from our own. It is a remarkable, colourful and intriguing place that you will remember for ever, not the least because of the superb riding experience.

Chamonix

This is the alpine capital of Europe and has a reputation that attracts the more serious aficionados of both winter and summer sports. In the northern part of the French alps, Chamonix is close to the borders of France, Italy and Switzerland. It is a beautiful, traditional town with a rich

history dedicated to mountain climbing, and the view from anywhere in the town is nothing short of breathtaking. Dramatic peaks, including the 15,866-ft (4808-m) Mont Blanc, surround the valley and glaciers fall to within 650ft (200m) of the town.

With the massive face of Mont Blanc dominating the

town, Chamonix is everything that the outdoor enthusiast could desire. Perfect for whatever winter or summer sport you may wish to try, Chamonix is full of all-round sports freaks who regard the valley as their extended playground. These are the people who spend their time doing crazy things which

include bungee jumping, parapenting, base jumping, riding bikes down bob-sled runs – they're all here.

As you might expect, therefore, mountain biking here is an awesome experience. Though the valley sides are steep there are fantastically varied terraced tracks all around that gently

OPPOSITE: In Chamonix, you can ride in the snow all-year-round!

BELOW: There are high mountains all around, but not so high that you cannot breathe.

BELOW RIGHT: The downhills seem to go on for ever, but there's often a cable car to take you back up to the top!

climb and descend, but mostly climb and climb, in some cases right up to the ridges. Like other ski-based resorts, it's not unusual to find snow on the trails right through the year.

At over 3,280ft (1000m) above sea level, you can't expect total trail access after the first big snowfalls (as early as October). From the town itself, there is very little immediate gravity-assisted riding, it's all up on the valley sides and peaks that loom above. If you don't like riding uphill, no matter, there's an extensive lift system to take you to the top. Most of the lifts will take bikes, but many of them close after the winter season for maintenance, re-opening in mid-June through to late September. Prices for one-way trips are moderate and bikes thankfully go free.

Expect a good quota of warm sunny days in summer, but always be prepared for occasional dramatic changes, especially high up in the mountains, as well as nocturnal storms. During early and late summer, the temperature drops at night, but shorts can still be worn in the evenings in July and August.

Nepal

Hugely popular with hippy tourists in the 1960s, Nepal has done well to reinvent itself as an adventure travel destination. Thousands flock here every year to 'café explore' and walk half-way up a path to where Everest begins. For the mountain biker who wishes to experience something a little different, it's popular, notably because there are some incredible trails and, best of all, some remarkable descents.

We're not talking world-class downhill standard trails here, but tracks that wander from village to village which enable you to spend the best part of a day going downhill,

make an overnight stop, and carry on the next day.

Kathmandu is the place from which to start, and where you can sort out all your needs: get your visas and permits sorted out here so that you can benefit the locals by putting money into their pockets rather than paying the inflated prices charged by a travel agent to do it from the comfort of their office.

Once you've obtained the right permits, it's simple to pick up information and advice and hit the trails whenever you feel like going.

Like Morocco, much of the best mountain biking is to be found on the access roads to the local villages, and on

the paths by which the locals travel about the countryside. Be courteous and polite and you'll have no problems. Be prepared to change your habits to fit in with the local way of doing things and you should have a great time.

ABOVE: Although Kathmandu is seen as a hippy location, it offers plenty of opportunity for the mountain biker.

RIGHT: Admiring the view of the 25,000-ft (7580-m) Porje Lakpa, a mountain in the Himalayas.

The descent from Tibet into Nepal. If you like downhilling, this one goes on for 44,620ft (13600m)!

Index

Glossary

Bearing This contains small balls that enable the moving parts to work smoothly. They are present in the wheel hub, pedals, headset and bottom bracket.

Bottom bracket This joins the seat tube to the downtube and houses the crank bearing. The crank joins the pedal to the bottom bracket and gear system.

Brake blocks These are pads that grip the wheel to stop it once the brake is applied.

'Clipless' pedal (see Toe clip)

Derailleur A gear system found on many bikes that pushes the chain across the sprockets or chainwheels when a shift lever is moved. Also known as the 'mech'.

Dropout The plate welded to the frame or forks, where the wheels fit into the frame.

Front mech The part of the derailleur gear system that is fixed to the seat tube. It moves the chain from one chainring to another.

Headset The bearing in which the fork steerer tube rotates, contained in the headtube.

Hub This forms the centre part of the wheel and has bearings and an axle which allow the wheel to turn.

Mech (see Derailleur).

Rear mech The part of the derailleur gear system that is fixed to the right-hand rear dropout. It moves the chain from one sprocket to another.

Seat Post The tube that is clamped into the frame and supports the saddle.

Shimano The Japanese component manufacturer which has almost total market dominance on production bikes and makes good, reliable equipment.

Shifters The levers on the handlebar which allow you to change gear.

Spokes Thin rods that runs from the hub to the outer rim of the wheel.

Stem The tube that attaches the handlebars to the headset.

Titanium Wonder metal of the modern age which is sometimes used in cycle frames, along with other exotic metals, and which is light and strong though very expensive.

Toe clip A device attached to the pedal which is designed to keep your foot in the right place. The 'clipless' pedal has a mechanical 'ski-binding' system which clips to a compatible shoe via a metal cleat bolted into the shoe's sole.

Tyre lever A tool which allows you to part the tyre from the wheel rim.

Valve Situated on the inner tube of the tyre, this is the means by which you can either pump in or release air from the tyre.